Way out!

Doctor, doctor can you please help me out?

Yes, over there—the same way that you came i

Monster dot-to-dot

Connect the dots to complete the picture.

How do you speak to a monster?
Very politely.

Radio Ant

How does an ant send messages to her friends?

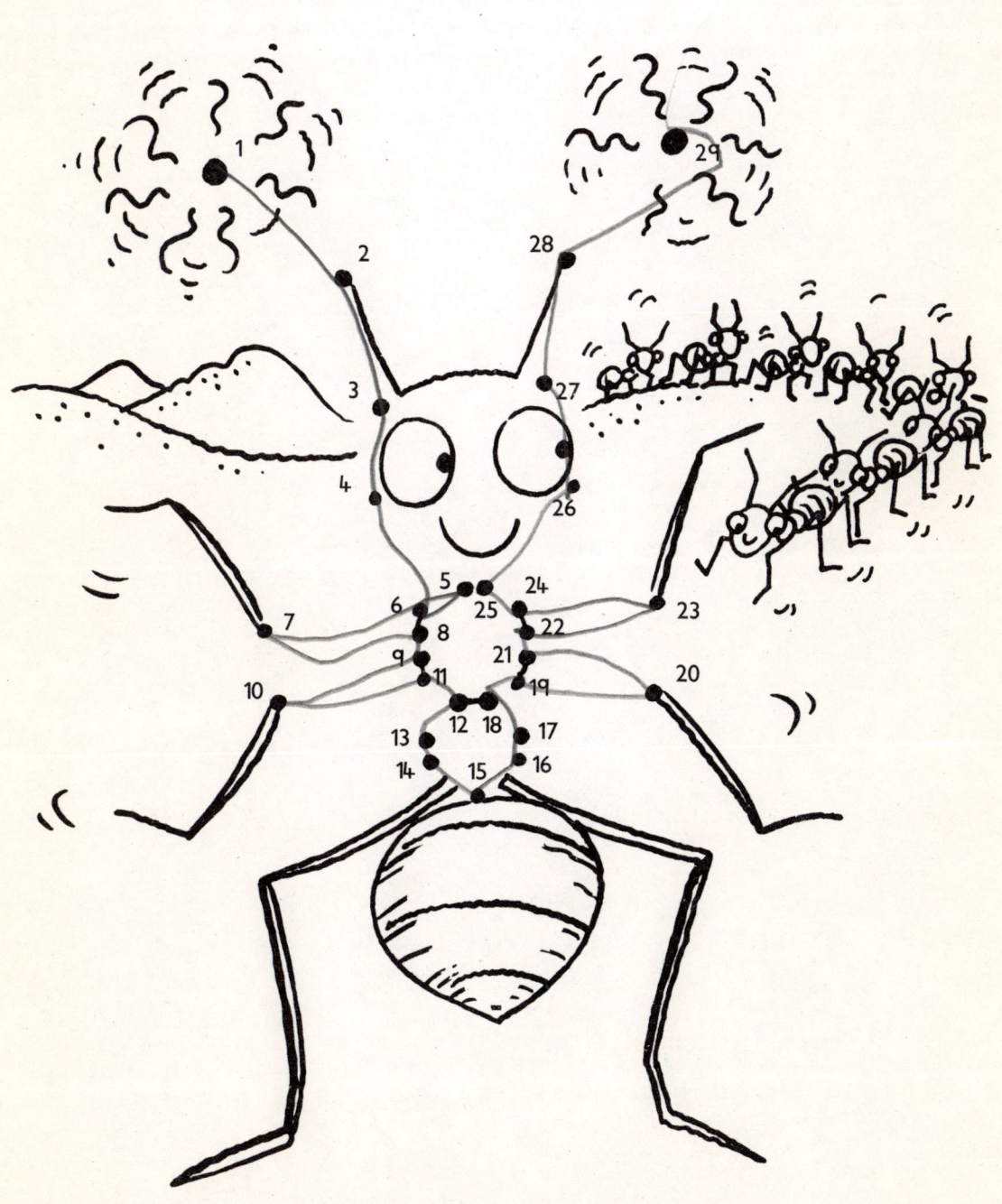

She uses her ANTennae.

Answer on page 93

Color the picture

Grannie: Why haven't you eaten all your sprouts? When I was your age I ate everything!
Little girl: Do you still like sprouts?
Grannie: Yes!

Little girl: Well you eat them!

Mousey picture

Use colored pencils, felt-tip pens or paint to finish the picture.

Cow tale

Where do cowboys get their cows?

MOO YORK!

Flying tonight?

Who were the first brothers not to invent the airplane?

The WRONG brothers.
Connect the dots to complete the picture.

Answer on page 93

Coloring

What do you call a slug?

A homeless snail!

Brain teaser

What is the last thing to pass through a fly's mind as it crashes into a windscreen?

Its bottom!

Hair brained

Mommy, mommy why do the kids call me werewolf?

Quiet darling and comb your face!

Soup tales

Waiter, waiter what's this fly doing in my soup?

Looks like the breast stroke to me, Madam! Mmm... mind you
it could be the crawl as he looks a bit tired!

Answer on page 93

Electrifying!

What did the world's worst plumber do?

He fitted a plug to a bath!

Count its teeth

How can you tell how old a snake is?

If it's got a rattle – then it's a baby.

Batty

Why is cricket a vampire's favorite game?

Because they never run out of bats!

Dotty cat

What is the cat in 'The Jungle Book' called?

Meowgli!
Connect the dots to complete the picture.

Answer on page 94

Stars

Who is Dracula's favorite film star?

Bat Pitt

Chicken

Why did the chewing gum cross the road?

It was stuck to the chicken's foot.

Keyed up

Why is it so difficult to open a piano?

Because the keys are inside!
Connect the dots to complete the picture.

Answer on page 94

Get set

Can you sort out this puzzle? Brian, John, Dave and Raul are in a race. Raul finished as many places behind Dave as John was in front of Brian. Dave was not first and Brian was not second. Can you work out in which order they finished the race?

I think that _____ was first, _____ second, _____ third, and _____ was last.

Answer on page 96

Sad story

Why didn't the skeleton want to go to the party?

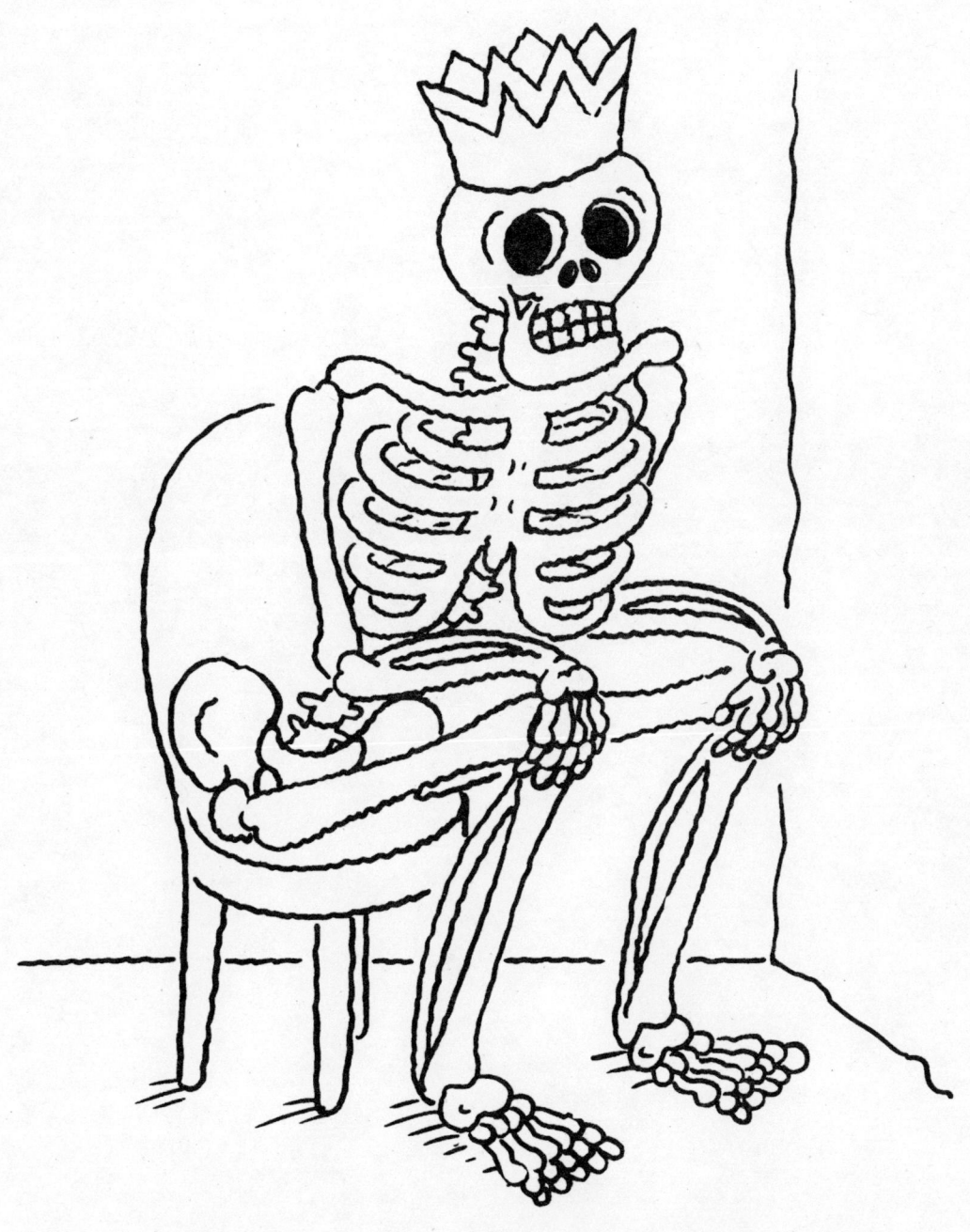

Because it had no body to go with!

Oh brother!

Why has your brother got ridges on his forehead?

He's my step brother!

Pie in the sky

What do the children of Italy dream of eating?

The Leaning Tower of Pizza!

Geography lesson

What is the capital of Italy?

'I'

Musical note

What does Neptune use to tune his piano?

A Tuna Fork!

Energy efficient

Why are electricians all slim?

Because they stick to light lunches!

It's not nice

Why do fishes go 'gloop, gloop'?

GLOOP GLOOP!

GLOOP GLOOP!

Because if they went 'Poop, Poop' it would be rude.
Connect the dots to complete the picture.

Answer on page 94

Ant time

What does the Pink Panther say when he treads on an ant?

Dead ant, dead ant, dead ant dead ant dead ant...

Fairy tale

Which movie frightened Tinker Bell most?

Nightmare on Elf Street!

Favorites

What is Dracula's favorite TV programme?

Bat Watch!

Convenient

Why did the Zombie move into the morgue?

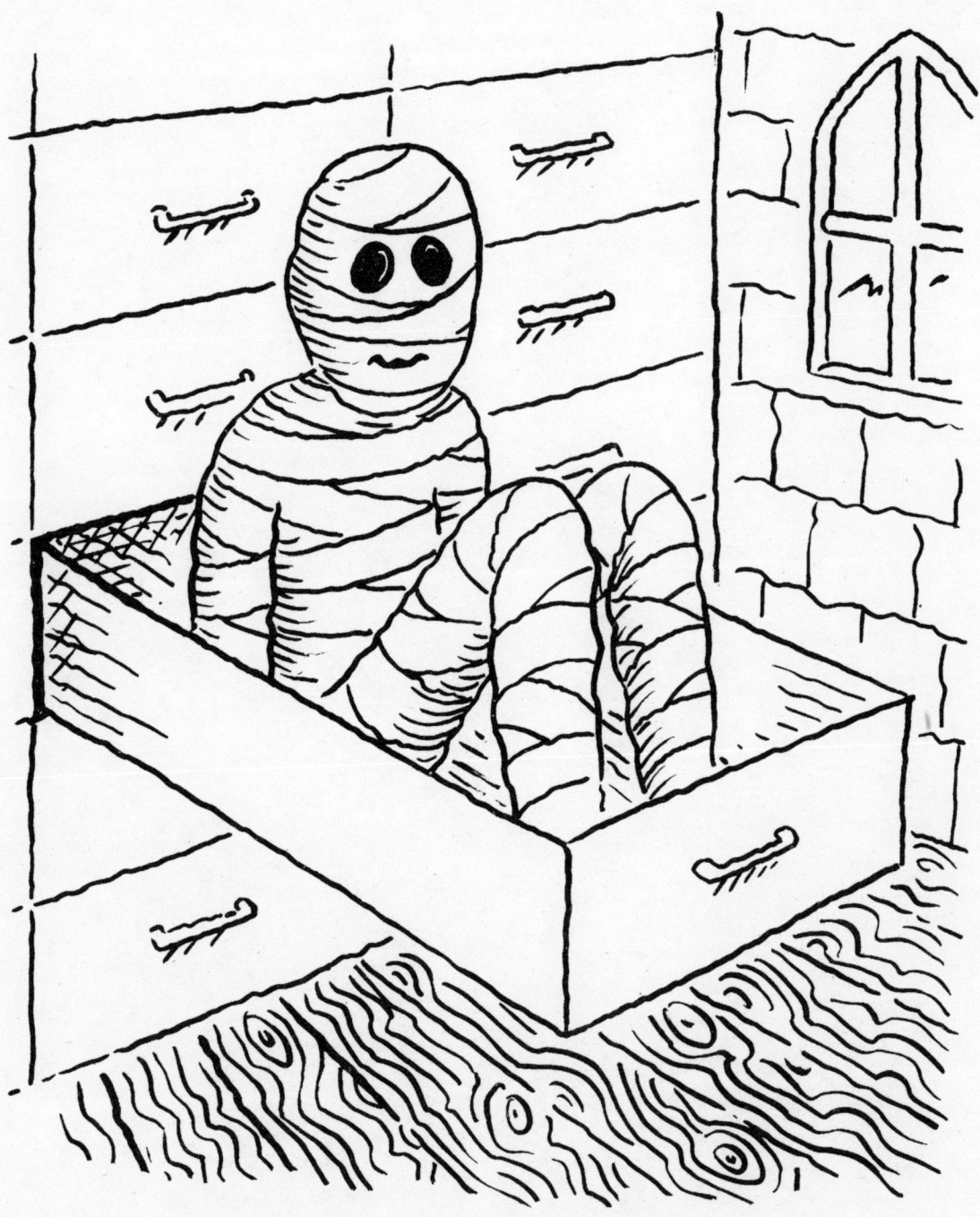

Because it was the dead centre of town!

Mind your own business!

Knock-knock. Who's there? Scot. Scot who?

Scot nothing to do with you!

Useful tales

What sort of snakes can you find on cars?

Windscreen Vipers!

Clues

Dracula's mummy was murdered. Who investigated the crime?

Sherlock Bones!

Warm story

What do bald men do to keep their ears warm?

They wear Ear Wigs!

Warm story

What do bald men do to keep their ears warm?

They wear Ear Wigs!

Soapy story

What is a monster's favorite TV show?

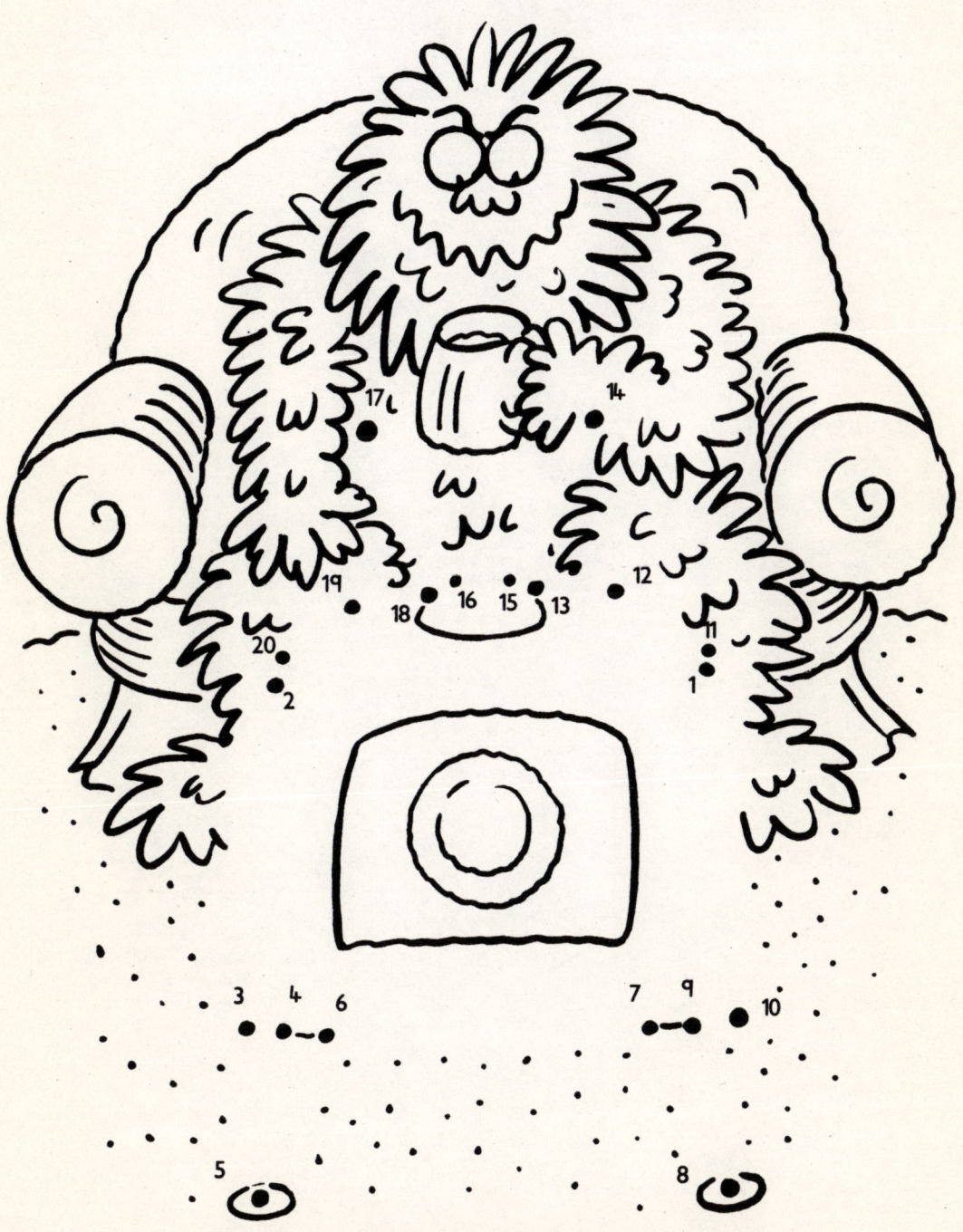

Fiends!
Connect the dots to complete the picture.

Answer on page 94

Soapy story

What is a monster's favorite TV show?

Planet

Connect the dots to complete the picture

Speechless

What happened to the pig that lost its voice?

It was disGruntled!

Speechless

What happened to the pig that lost its voice?

It was disGruntled.

Rhyming pictures

Hidden in this picture are eight things. The names rhyme to make four pairs. One name is GRATE, can you find the others and match them?

The rhyming pairs are GRATE and _____,
_____ and _____, _____ and _____,
and _____ and _____.

Answer on page 96

Cheeky

Who was the first Scottish man?

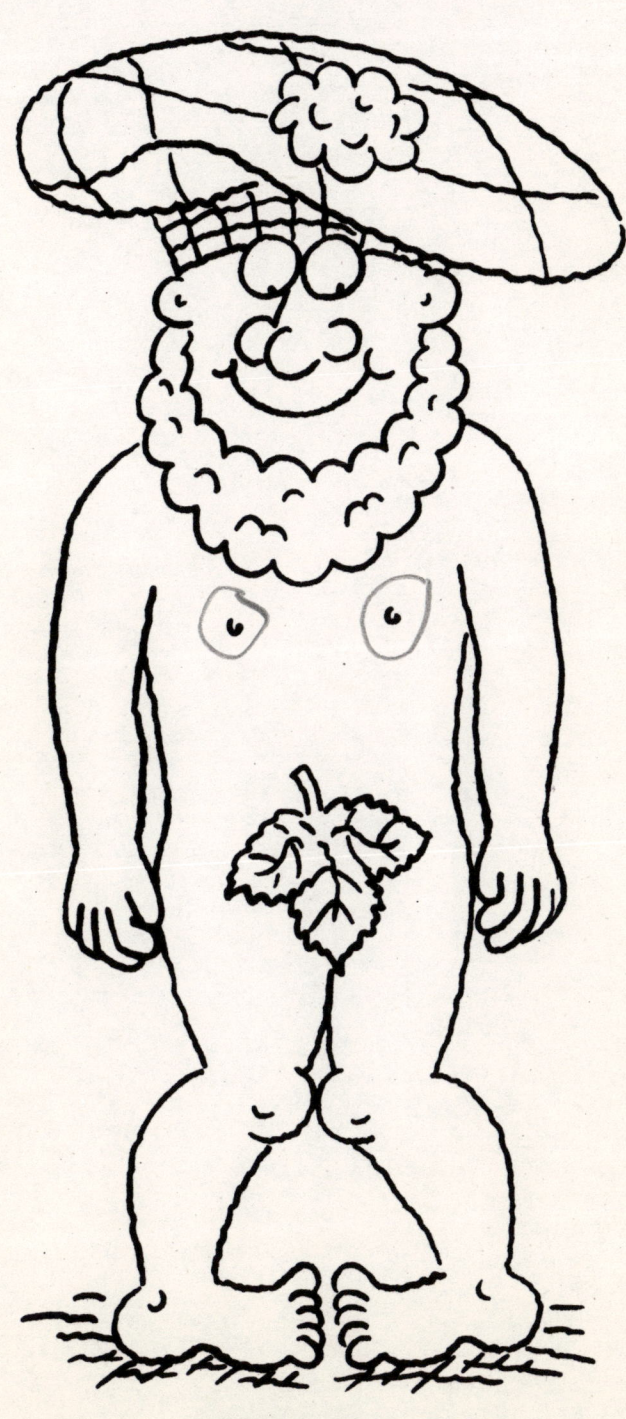

MacAdam!

Cheeky

Who was the first Scottish man?

MacAdam!

Beach wear

What sort of shoes do frogs wear on the beach?

Open toad sandals!

Beach wear

What sort of shoes do frogs wear on the beach?

Open toad shoes!

Close eye-counter

Mommy, mommy how is it that kids call me four eyes?

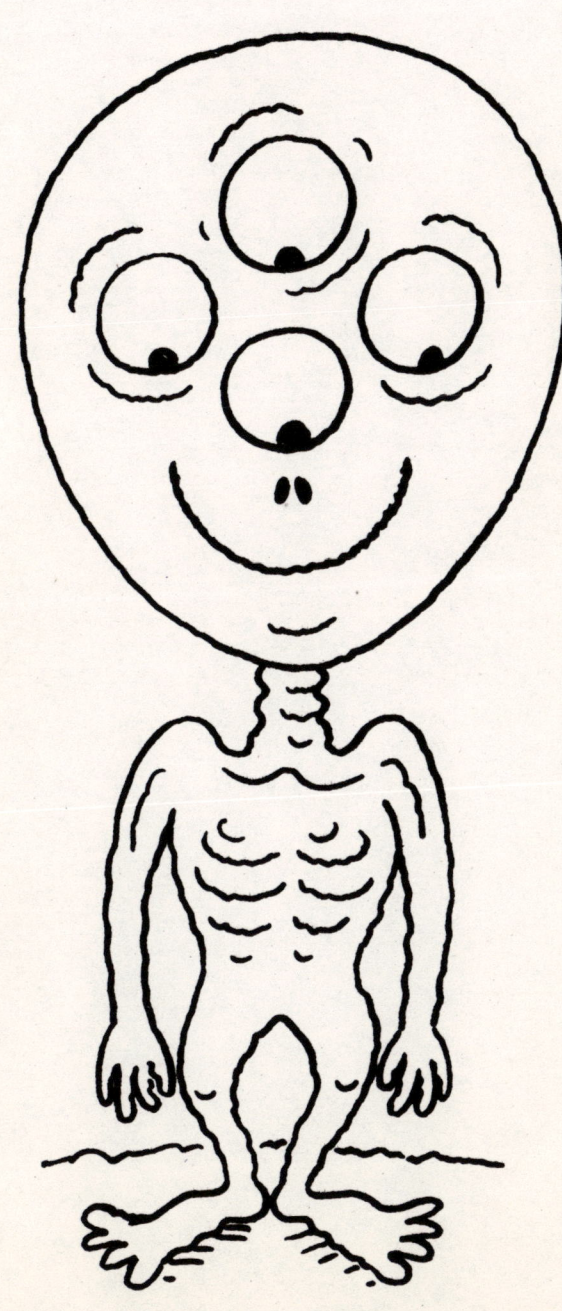

Eye, eye, eye, eye!

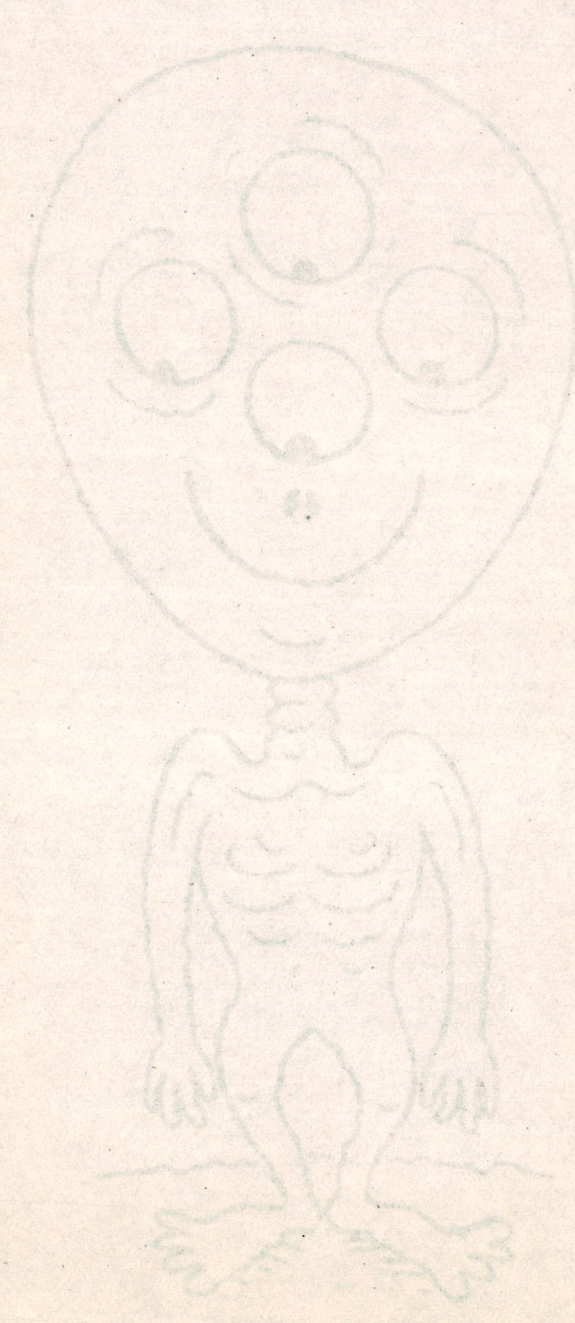

Holiday horror

You are going to the seaside, but the train is crowded and you get bumped and jostled all the way. What could you suffer from riding on such overcrowded TRAINS? (Try rearranging the letters).

I think that you could suffer from _____

Answer on page 96

Crushing

What did the grape do when the elephant stood on it?

It just let out a little wine!
Connect the dots to complete the picture.

Answer on page 95

Fair

At the fair which race always starts with a tie?

I think it is the _____

Tall story

What's the tallest building in Transylvania?

The Vampire State Building.
Connect the dots to complete the picture.

Poor Miss

Have you heard the one about the cross-eyed teacher?

Sad really — she had no control over her pupils!

What's in a name?

What is huge, smelly, scary and hairy?

King Pong!

Cold

Knock, knock!
Who's there?
Trisha.
Trisha who?

Bless you!

Lessons

Teacher: Now children watch the board while I run through it again!

Sad tale

Mary had a little lamb—
She took it to the shop;
It was nice to have a little walk—

Before it had the chop!

Higher or hire?

How do you hire a taxi?

Put a brick under each wheel!

In the kitchen

How do you keep flies out of the kitchen?

Place a bucket of manure in every other room!

Hard-headed?

What do you call a man under a car?

Jack!

Noisy Brucie

Knock, knock!
Who's there?
Noise
Noise who?

Noise to see you, to see you noise!

Off the menu

Why don't sharks eat penguins?

Because they find the wrappers difficult!

Doctor, doctor

Oh doctor please help me! My hair is falling out everywhere.
Can you give me something for it?

Yes! Here, put it in this bin!

Coach trip

In 1492 which bus crossed the Atlantic?

Christopher ColumBUS

Stranded

Which island is like a box?

Cuba!

Hot water

Who is the most famous Roman plumber?

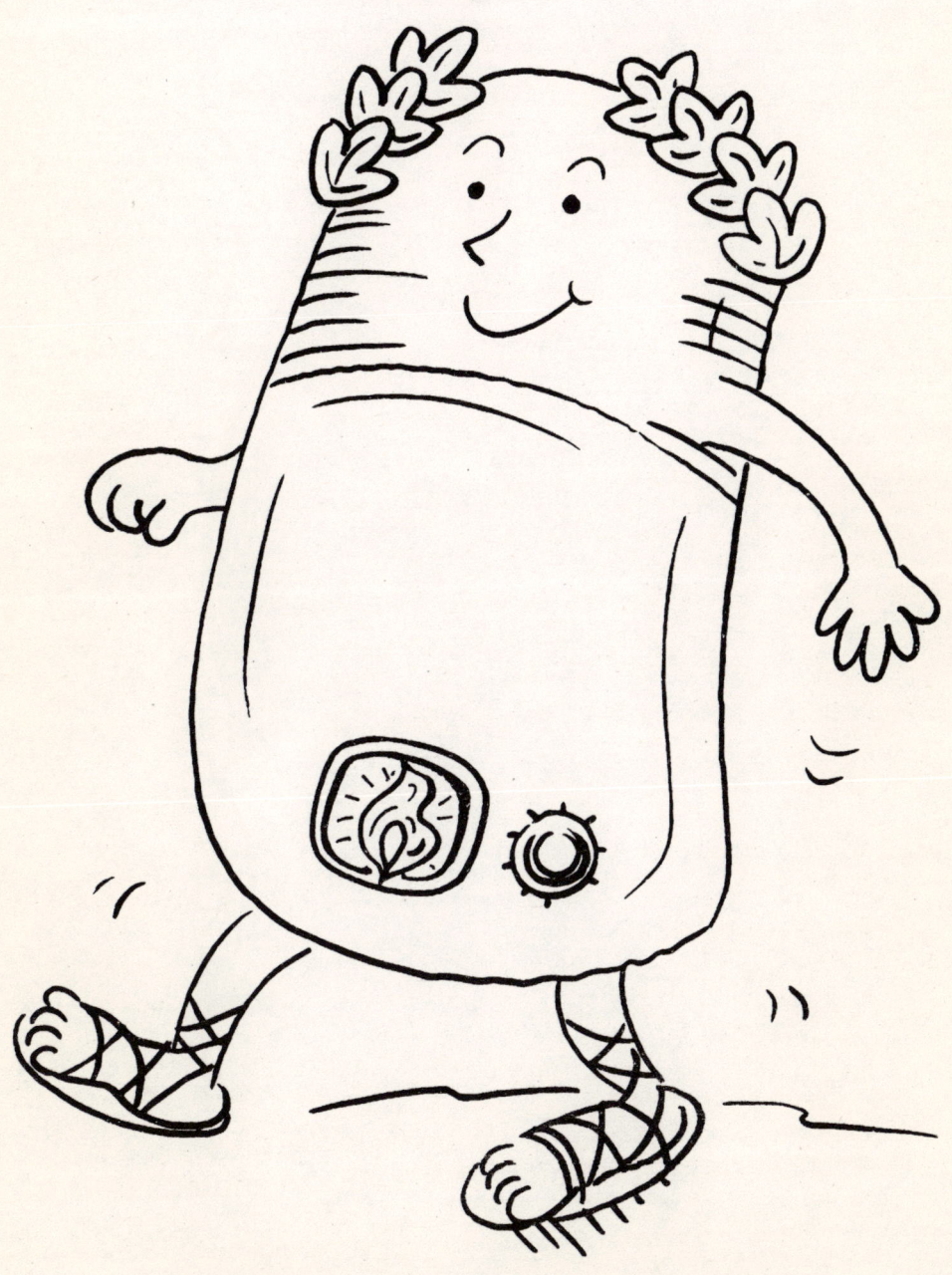

Julius Geezer.

Geography lesson

Teacher: Ronald, can you tell me where the Andes are?

Ronald: At the end of your wristies?

Sea sighed

What does the sea say to the beach?

Not much – it mostly just waves.

Hot stuff

What happened to the monster who had too hot a curry?

He spent a week Vindaloo!

Ghoulish

What is the difference between a man and his ghost?

The man is all grown while his ghost is all groan!

High Q

Of all the animals, which has the highest brain power?

The Giraffe!
Connect the dots to complete the picture.

Answer on page 95

Baldy

Why did the bald man keep a rabbit on his head?

Because, from a distance it looked like a little hare!

Hole–Ho!

What is worse than finding a worm in your apple?

Finding a worm hole!

Rockaby ET

How do you get baby ET to sleep?

Rock-ET

Diets

My sister is on a Seafood diet.

As soon as she sees food she eats it.

Sniff sniff

What is yellow and sniffs?

A banana with the flu!

Beauty prize

My sister won second prize in a beauty contest.

Yes, there was only a monkey and her there!

Big, bigger and biggest

What's the biggest ant in the world called?

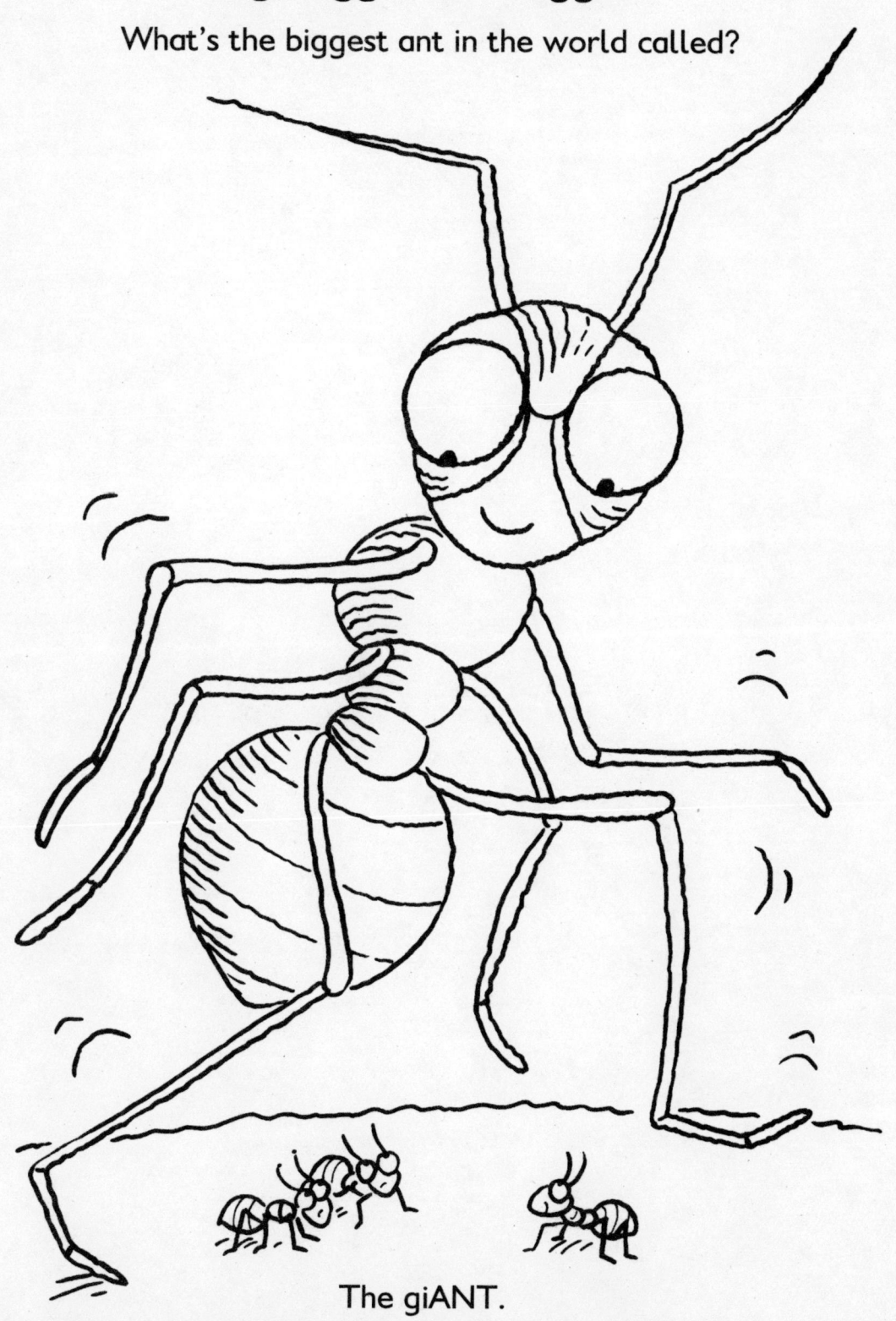

The giANT.

Favorites

Who is Dracula's favorite Jungle-Swinging hero?

Batzan!

Breakfast time

What do the Addams family have for breakfast?

Buttered Ghost and a little Ghoul tea.

Go South

Why do birds fly south for the winter?

Because they can't walk on water!

I spied a spider

What has eight legs and flies?

A spider in an airplane.

Cat knap

What does a cat rest its head on?

A Caterpillar.
Connect the dots to complete the picture.

Answer on page 95

Well, well!

On which side of a turkey do you find most feathers?

On the outside!

Lonely Ice

Why did the ice cream cornet cry?

Because its mom had been a waifer too long.

Mythology

What is a female moth called?

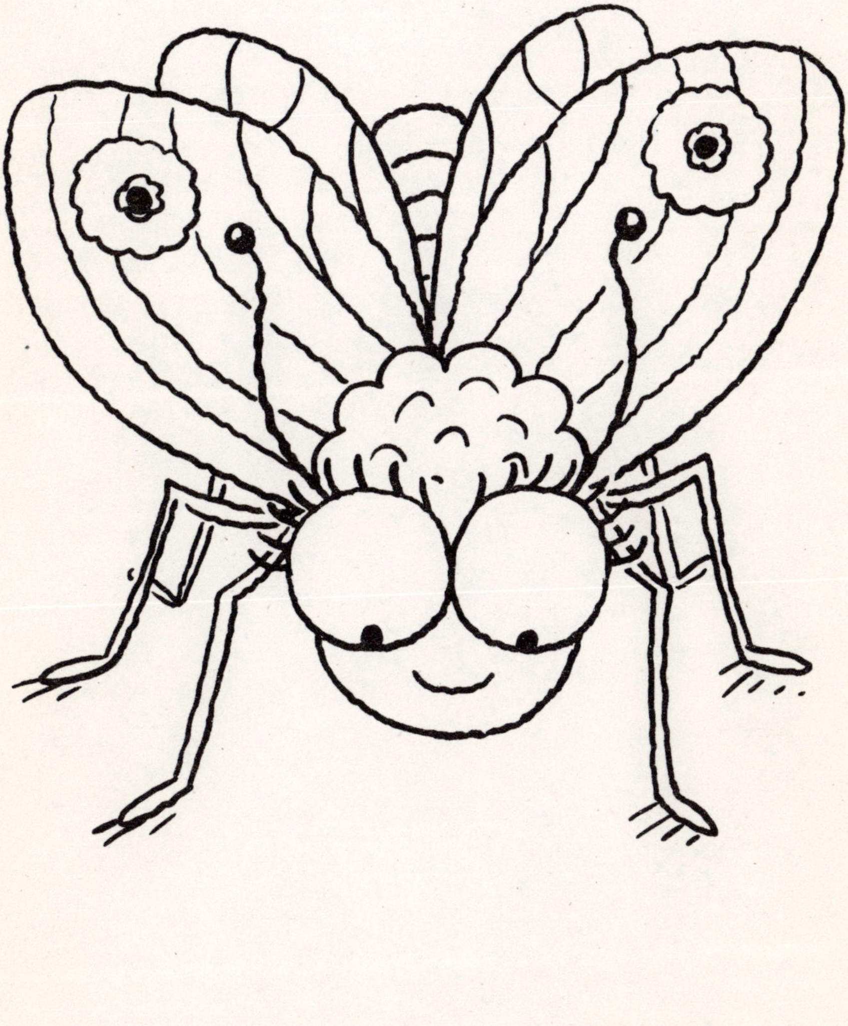

A myth!

Tired?

Which bird is always out of breath?

A Puffin.

Gnasher, gnasher

Knock, knock!
Who's there?
Adair
Adair who?

Adair you to open the door and see my teeth!

Animal crackers

What sort of fish do dogs chase?

Catfish!

Stopping shopping

How do you stop a rhino charging?

Take away its credit card.

Cross road

Why did the hedgehog cross the road?

To see her flatmate.

Dream team

Who is Dracula's favorite footballer?

David Neckham!

Gutsy Girl

Which little girl scared away the Three Bears?

Ghouldilocks.

Home alone

Where in your house would you hide to avoid an unwelcome CALLER? Find out by rearranging the letters.

Answer on page 96

Fish

What happened after the jellyfish got married?

They had jello babies.

Be tidy

Why do bees always have messy hair?

Because they insist on only using honey combs!

Sheepish joke

When is a sheep like ink?

When it's in a pen!

Sick or not?

Why shouldn't you trust this person?

Because he is obviously lying!

More milk please

If the mommy cow can give 4 litres of milk a day and the young cow can give 3 litres, how many litres can the daddy cow give a day?

Answer on page 96

More milk please

If one mamma cow can give 4 litres of milk a day and the
baby cow can give 2 litres how many litres can the baby
cow give a day?

Cats and dogs

Which line contains all these letters – c, a, t, d, o, g and s?

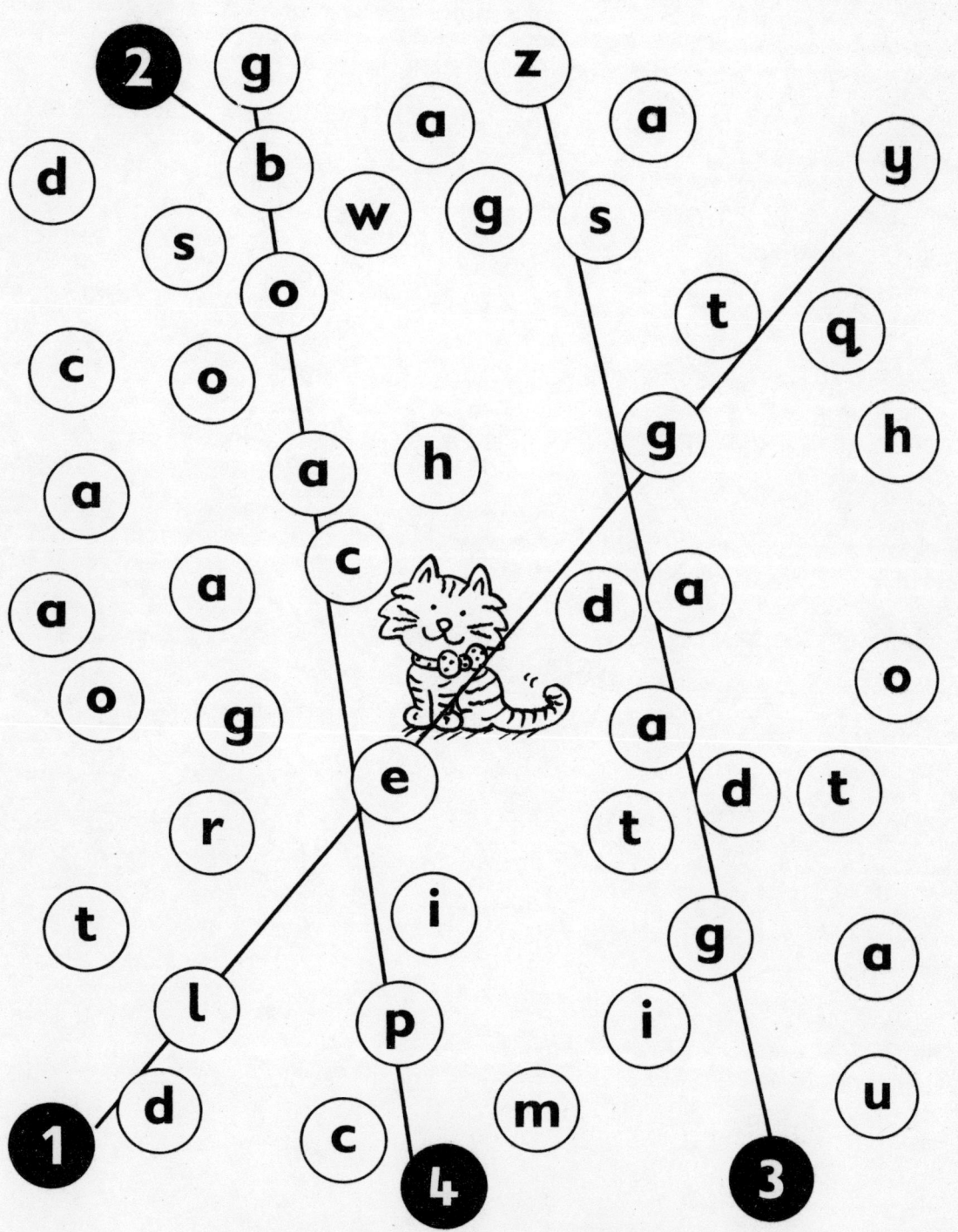

The line that has all the letters is ___

Answer on page 96

Answers (all the dot-to-dots are shown first, then all the other answers are given - those not obvious from the page).

1 Monster dot-to-dot

3 Radio Ant

7 Flying tonight?

11 Soup tales

Answers

15 Dotty cat

18 Keyed up

26 It's not nice

35 Soapy story

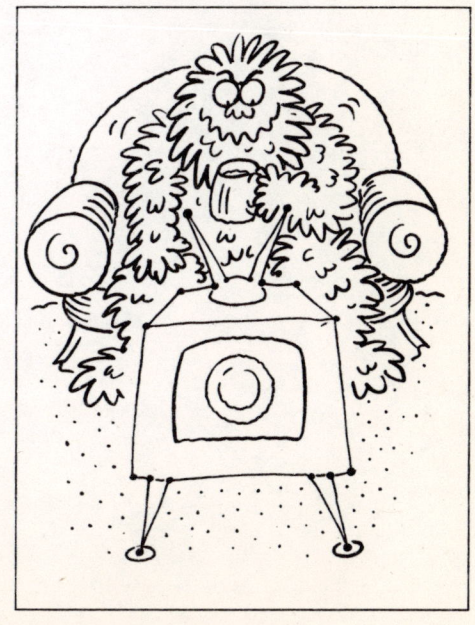

Answers

42 Crushing

44 Tall story

63 High Q

75 Cat knap

Answers

Page

19 **Get set:** JOHN came first, then DAVE, BRIAN and last was RAUL

37 **Rhyming pictures:** the rhyming pictures are – GRATE and PLATE, PIG and WIG, MUG and JUG, HEN and PEN

41 **Holiday horror:** TRAINS can give you STRAIN

43 **Fair:** the THREE-LEGGED race starts with a tie!

86 **Home alone:** you could hide in the CELLAR

91 **More milk please:** THE DADDY COW does not give any milk; it is a BULL!

92 **Cats and dogs:** the line that contains all of C, A, T, D, O, G and S is number 4